BREAKOUT BIOGRAPHIES

LIN-MANUEL MIRANDA

Award-Winning Actor, Rapper, Writer, and Composer

Theresa Morlock

PowerKiDS
press.

New York

Published in 2018 by The Rosen Publishing Group, Inc.
29 East 21st Street, New York, NY 10010

First Edition

Editor: Elizabeth Krajnik
Book Design: Tanya Dellaccio

Photo Credits: Cover Jeff Kravitz/FilmMagic, Inc/Getty Images; p. 5 Craig Barritt/
Getty Images Entertainment/Getty Images; p. 7 (top) Walter McBride/WireImage/Getty Images;
p. 7 (bottom) Carolyn Cole/Los Angeles Times/Getty Images; p. 9 (top) William Thomas Cain/
Getty Images Entertainment/Getty Images; pp. 9 (bottom), 29 (top) Dimitrios Kambouris/Getty Images
Entertainment/Getty Images; p. 11 (top) Chelsea Lauren/Getty Images Entertainment/Getty Images;
p. 11 (bottom) Steven A Henry/WireImage/Getty Images; p. 13 Evan Agostini/Invision/AP Images;
p. 15 (top) Gary Gershoff/Getty Images Entertainment/Getty Images; p. 15 (bottom) Cindy Ord/
Getty Images Entertainment/Getty Images; p. 17 (top) Nicholas Hunt/Getty Images Entertainment/
Getty Images; pp. 17 (bottom), 19 (both) Theo Wargo/Getty Images Entertainment/Getty Images;
p. 21 NICHOLAS KAMM/AFP/Getty Images; p. 23 (top) Alberto E. Rodriguez/Getty Images
Entertainment/Getty Images; p. 23 (bottom) Jesse Grant/Getty Images Entertainment/Getty Images;
p. 25 TIMOTHY A. CLARY/AFP/Getty Images; p. 27 Mark Sagliocco/Getty Images Entertainment/
Getty Images; p. 29 (bottom) Jamie McCarthy/Getty Images Entertainment/Getty Images.

Cataloging-in-Publication Data

Names: Morlock, Theresa.
Title: Lin-Manuel Miranda: award-winning actor, rapper, writer, and composer / Morlock, Theresa.
Description: New York : PowerKids Press, 2018. | Series: Breakout biographies | Includes index.
Identifiers: LCCN ISBN 9781538326244 (pbk.) | ISBN 9781538325551 (library bound) | ISBN
9781538326251 (6 pack)
Subjects: LCSH: Miranda, Lin-Manuel, 1980–Juvenile literature. | Actors–United States–Biography–Juvenile
literature. | Composers–United States–Biography–Juvenile literature. | Lyricists–United States–Biography–Juvenile
literature.
Classification: LCC PN2287.M6446 M8417 2018 | DDC 792.02'8092 B–dc23

Manufactured in the United States of America

CPSIA Compliance Information: Batch #BW18PK For Further Information contact Rosen Publishing, New York, New York at 1-800-237-9932

CONTENTS

NONSTOP!

Lin-Manuel Miranda has been described as quick, bright, gifted, charming, inventive, magnetic, and much more! His dynamic personality is only part of what makes him so special. Miranda has achieved great fame in a short time. His skills as a poet, performer, rapper, composer, and writer have earned him worldwide recognition.

Miranda's parents are of Puerto Rican descent, and his **multicultural** upbringing has influenced his work. Miranda is best known for his Broadway musicals *In the Heights* and *Hamilton*, both of which he created and starred in. He's also the creator and a member of Freestyle Love Supreme. Miranda's work has earned him a number of awards, including the Pulitzer Prize for Drama in 2016. This man is working and creating nonstop!

Miranda has been praised for his immense creativity.

THE MIRANDA FAMILY

Miranda was born on January 16, 1980, in New York City. His mother, Luz, is a **psychologist** and his father, Luis, is a political consultant. His older sister is also named Luz. Miranda grew up in Inwood, a largely Hispanic neighborhood in northern Manhattan.

Throughout his childhood, Miranda's parents instilled a love of music in their children. Even though the family couldn't afford to go to Broadway shows often, they listened to their favorite musicals' soundtracks. His father particularly liked *The Unsinkable Molly Brown*. Miranda also listened to hip-hop on his bus ride to school. He attended Hunter College Elementary School, a school for gifted children, where he sang in the choir. He also took piano lessons.

LUZ MIRANDA

LUIS MIRANDA

During his 2016 acceptance speech for the Edward M. Kennedy Prize for drama inspired by American history, Miranda said, "I grew up in an **immigrant** neighborhood. We just knew the rule was you're going to have to work twice as hard."

A TALENTED YOUTH

Miranda started to perform in musicals when he was in sixth grade. In high school, he performed in *The Pirates of Penzance* and *Godspell*, helped direct *A Chorus Line*, and directed *West Side Story*. He enjoyed rock musicals and was particularly influenced by *Rent*. During his high school years, Miranda wrote two original musicals: *Nightmare in D Major* and *Seven Minutes in Heaven*.

Miranda went to Wesleyan University to study film and theater. However, he later stopped studying film to focus on theater. While at Wesleyan, he performed the role of Jesus in *Jesus Christ Superstar* and directed a **version** of his play *Seven Minutes in Heaven*. He also began writing a new musical, which he titled *In the Heights*.

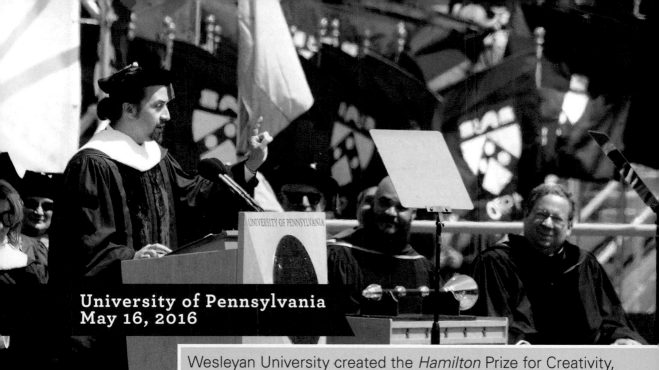

**University of Pennsylvania
May 16, 2016**

Wesleyan University created the *Hamilton* Prize for Creativity, which is a four-year full-tuition **scholarship** in honor of Miranda. He graduated from the university in 2002 and received an honorary doctorate ir 2015. In 2016, Miranda received an honorary doctorate from the University of Pennsylvania.

TO TEACH OR TO WRITE

After Miranda graduated from Wesleyan, he became a high school English teacher. He worked as a substitute and was offered several full-time teaching jobs. Miranda decided to put his energy into writing instead. He knew he had to follow his dream. He wasn't throwing away his shot. Miranda said his father told him: "It makes no sense to leave your job to be a writer, but I have to tell you to do it. You have to pursue that if you want."

IN THE HEIGHTS

Miranda started writing *In the Heights* when he was a sophomore in college. *Rent* showed Miranda that he could write a musical about current events and personal experiences. He didn't finish writing the musical until eight years later!

In the Heights is a story about people living in Washington Heights, a Latino neighborhood in Manhattan. The music, which Miranda composed and wrote lyrics for, has Latin and hip-hop influences.

In the Heights premiered, or was performed for the public for the first time, on Broadway in March 2008. The show ran for two years and won four Tony Awards, including those for best musical and best original score. In 2009, *In the Heights* was nominated for the Pulitzer Prize for Drama and won the Grammy Award for best musical show album.

THE STORY

In the Heights takes place over three days. The main characters are Usnavi, Vanessa, Nina, and Benny. Usnavi, played by Miranda, owns a **bodega**. Usnavi's dream is to one day return to his home country—the Dominican Republic. In 2008, Miranda was nominated for the Tony Award for best performance by a leading actor in a musical for his role as Usnavi. *In the Heights* is inspired by Miranda's experiences growing up. He expressed the feeling of having a foot in two **cultures** as a Latino American.

In the Heights is a two-and-a-half-hour, two-act musical about chasing your dreams.

AFTER THE HEIGHTS

After *In the Heights*'s great success, Miranda continued to work hard. He did Spanish translations for the 2009 revival of *West Side Story*. He co-composed and co-wrote lyrics for *Bring It On: The Musical* in 2012. Miranda also guest starred on TV shows including *How I Met Your Mother*, *Modern Family*, and *The Sopranos*.

While writing and performing, Miranda also helped create a comedy and improvisation group called Freestyle Love Supreme. Improvisation is a style of performance in which the actors create short scenes or pieces of music on the spot, with no preparation. Freestyle Love Supreme is made up of five performers including Miranda. They perform hip-hop and improvised music and scenes at festivals and colleges across the country.

On March 6, 2014, Freestyle Love Supreme took part in a live taping of their show. Pictured here from right are Miranda, Arthur Lewis, Chris Jackson, Anthony Veneziale, and Utkarsh Ambudkar.

PERSONAL LIFE

Miranda met Vanessa Nadal, the woman who would later become his wife, while he was in high school. He was a senior at Hunter College High School when Nadal was a sophomore. Although they weren't friends in school, Miranda was always interested in Nadal, who grew up in Washington Heights.

While Miranda was at Wesleyan University, Nadal attended Massachusetts Institute of Technology. The two didn't come into contact again until 2005, when Miranda came across her profile when he was catching up with graduates from Hunter College High School on Facebook. He learned that Nadal was a scientist working at Johnson & Johnson. He invited her to see his upcoming Freestyle Love Supreme show. She came to the show and the two started dating soon after. They were married on September 5, 2010.

At their wedding, Miranda surprised Nadal by performing the song "To Life" from *Fiddler on the Roof*.

LIFE AS A FATHER

On November 10, 2014, Nadal and Miranda welcomed their son Sebastian into the world. During the first year of Sebastian's life, Miranda was often away performing *Hamilton*. Miranda credits his wife with keeping their family running smoothly. He stated: "My wife's the reason anything gets done." By the time he was just two years old, Sebastian was already bilingual, speaking Spanish and English. Miranda has said that Sebastian is working on learning a third language. Miranda's mother-in-law is Austrian and has taught Sebastian some German.

CREATING *HAMILTON*

In 2008, Miranda picked up a biography, or written history of a person's life, of Alexander Hamilton by Ron Chernow. As he read, he was inspired by Chernow's explanation of Hamilton's personality and life story. He felt that the story of the nation's first secretary of the treasury needed to be told.

Miranda spent the next few years composing and writing a musical **concept** album based on Chernow's biography of Hamilton. He turned to hip-hop to bring the story to life, describing it as "the language of youth and energy and of **rebellion**," which made it a perfect fit for a story about the American Revolution. It took Miranda a year to write the first song and another year to finish the second. *The Hamilton Mixtape* would eventually become the Broadway musical *Hamilton*.

Chernow said that Miranda's musical is "a biographer's wish-fulfillment **fantasy**."

In 2009, Miranda was invited to perform at the White House's Evening of Poetry and Spoken Word. Miranda chose to perform a song from *The Hamilton Mixtape*, which hadn't been released yet. On January 11, 2012, Miranda gave the audience at the American Songbook series at Lincoln Center in New York City a sneak preview of 12 songs from *The Hamilton Mixtape*.

When casting *Hamilton* when it became a musical, Miranda chose actors based on their abilities, regardless of whether they looked like the historical figures they played. Miranda said, "I think our goal is to present them as human, and not just the five facts you know about them from our history books." *Hamilton* premiered at the Public Theater in New York City in 2015.

THE MACARTHUR FOUNDATION AWARD

On September 28, 2015, Miranda received the MacArthur Foundation Award and Genius Grant. A grant is an award of financial support that's given to an individual or organization. The John D. and Catherine T. MacArthur Foundation is an organization that focuses on supporting creative projects and talented artists. The MacArthur Foundation awarded Miranda a grant of $625,000 to support his continuing creative projects.

Hamilton received rave reviews from theatergoers. *New York Times* writer Ben Brantley wrote that *Hamilton* is "proof that the American musical is not only surviving but also evolving in ways that should allow it to **thrive**."

HAMILTON'S
SUCCESS

Hamilton immediately became a huge hit. The 2015 off-Broadway production of *Hamilton* at the Public Theater sold out 119 shows. Many celebrities and politicians saw the show, including Madonna, Dick Cheney, and Jake Gyllenhaal.

When *Hamilton* moved to Broadway, over 200,000 tickets were sold in advance, bringing total advance ticket sales to almost $30 million!

In 2016, *Hamilton* was nominated for 16 Tony Awards, of which it took home 11. Miranda himself was awarded a Tony for best score, best book of a musical, and best musical. *Hamilton* also won awards for best leading actor, best featured actor, best featured actress, best **choreography**, best costume design, and more.

Hamilton also won the 2016 Pulitzer Prize for Drama and a Grammy Award for best musical theater album.

On March 14, 2016, the Broadway cast of *Hamilton* performed songs from the musical for President Barack Obama and others at the White House.

WRITING MUSIC FOR *MOANA*

In 2014, Miranda signed on with Disney to create songs for the computer-**animated** film *Moana*. He worked with Opetaia Tavita Foa'i and Mark Mancina. Foa'i was born in Samoa, which is part of Polynesia, where *Moana* takes place. His vocal group, Te Vaka, helped create the sounds of *Moana*. Mancina had helped write music for Disney's *Tarzan* and *Brother Bear*. The three men worked together to create the music for *Moana*.

Miranda told Variety, "We did a lot of jam sessions around drums. It would start with a rhythmic bass line from Opetaia, then I would go and write music and lyrics, and then he'd come in with choral stuff, and then Mark would make it feel all of a piece."

At *Moana*'s world premiere on November 14, 2016, Miranda and Dwayne Johnson performed a live version of "You're Welcome" from the movie.

"HOW FAR I'LL GO"

In 2017, Miranda was nominated for the Academy Award, or Oscar, for music (original song) for his work on "How Far I'll Go" from *Moana*. He performed the song at the Oscars with actress Auli'i Cravalho, who voiced *Moana* in the film. *Moana* was also nominated for the Oscar for best animated feature. *Moana* didn't win the Oscar in either category. The song "City of Stars" from the movie *La La Land* won the Oscar for music (original song).

AULI'I CRAVALHO

23

THE HAMILTON MIXTAPE

The Hamilton Mixtape, which was released in December 2016, is a collection of covers, reimaginings, and spin-offs of songs from the musical *Hamilton*. Miranda's first songs from the original *Hamilton Mixtape*, which was written before the musical was released, are included on the album.

While working on the album, Miranda said, "I'm really excited to sort of see how well these songs play in the pop, hip-hop music sphere—they actually work really well as radio tunes." The new *Mixtape* features songs by pop stars including Sia and Kelly Clarkson. Contributions from hip-hop musicians such as Nas, Chance the Rapper, and Common and performances by R&B musicians John Legend and Alicia Keys are also featured. A review by *Rolling Stone* said, "*Hamilton* is full of show tunes that feel as vital as anything in contemporary pop . . ."

On October 17, 2016, at the "Stronger Together" Broadway benefit for presidential candidate Hillary Clinton, Miranda remixed, or changed, the lyrics to the *Hamilton* song "The World Was Wide Enough." The new lyrics for the rap focused on Clinton and the importance of voting.

IMMIGRANTS:
WE GET THE JOB DONE

In 2017, the Hispanic Federation, a nonprofit Latino organization, and 12 other nonprofit organizations from across the United States came together to launch the Immigrants: We Get the Job Done **Coalition**. The coalition takes its name from lyrics from the song "Yorktown" from *Hamilton*. The coalition's goal is to protect and improve the rights of immigrants in the United States.

Miranda has said that working for immigrant rights is a cause close to his heart. In honor of Immigrant Heritage Month, Miranda started a campaign called the #Ham4All Challenge to raise money for the Immigrants: We Get the Job Done Coalition. He asked fans to donate to the coalition and post videos of themselves online performing songs from *Hamilton*. Those who participated were entered in a contest to win a chance to see *Hamilton* in Los Angeles.

KAREN OLIVO

Miranda helped create a video based on the song "Immigrants (We Get the Job Done)" from *The Hamilton Mixtape* to raise awareness of the issues many immigrants face in the United States. Actress Karen Olivo donated to the Immigrants: We Get the Job Done Coalition. She had roles in *In the Heights* and *Hamilton*.

WHAT COMES NEXT?

Lin-Manuel Miranda is a whirlwind of energy. He's created groundbreaking works of art and achieved remarkable success, all before the age of 40. His talent as an actor, rapper, writer, and composer has earned him multiple awards and respect as a creative genius. What will the future hold for this amazing artist?

In 2017, Miranda began working on a movie musical called *Mary Poppins Returns*. He was cast as Jack alongside Emily Blunt as Mary Poppins. He's also written several songs for a movie musical called *Vivo*, which will be released in 2020. Additionally, Miranda has started working on a live-action version of Disney's *The Little Mermaid* as well as a movie version of his Broadway musical *In the Heights*. It seems that there's no end in sight for Lin-Manuel Miranda!

On July 11, 2016, Miranda (pictured below) performed "Love Make the World Go Round" with Jennifer Lopez on NBC's *TODAY* show to benefit survivors of the Orlando Pulse nightclub shooting.

TIMELINE

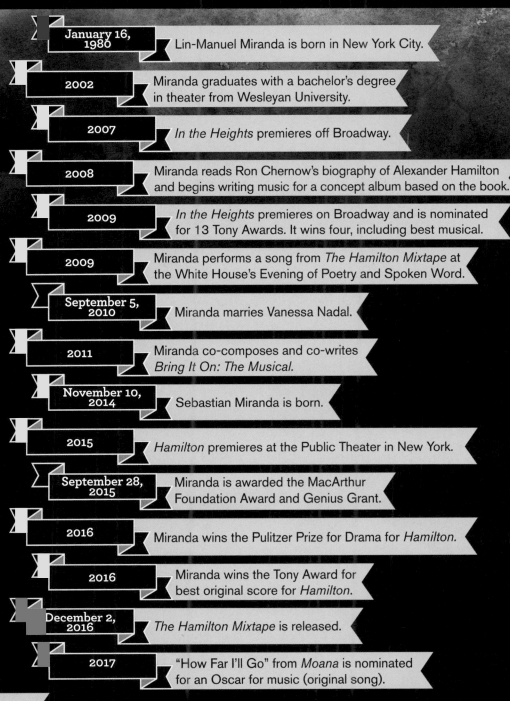

January 16, 1980	Lin-Manuel Miranda is born in New York City.
2002	Miranda graduates with a bachelor's degree in theater from Wesleyan University.
2007	*In the Heights* premieres off Broadway.
2008	Miranda reads Ron Chernow's biography of Alexander Hamilton and begins writing music for a concept album based on the book.
2009	*In the Heights* premieres on Broadway and is nominated for 13 Tony Awards. It wins four, including best musical.
2009	Miranda performs a song from *The Hamilton Mixtape* at the White House's Evening of Poetry and Spoken Word.
September 5, 2010	Miranda marries Vanessa Nadal.
2011	Miranda co-composes and co-writes *Bring It On: The Musical.*
November 10, 2014	Sebastian Miranda is born.
2015	*Hamilton* premieres at the Public Theater in New York.
September 28, 2015	Miranda is awarded the MacArthur Foundation Award and Genius Grant.
2016	Miranda wins the Pulitzer Prize for Drama for *Hamilton.*
2016	Miranda wins the Tony Award for best original score for *Hamilton.*
December 2, 2016	*The Hamilton Mixtape* is released.
2017	"How Far I'll Go" from *Moana* is nominated for an Oscar for music (original song).

GLOSSARY

animated: Produced by a series of drawings or pictures that are shown quickly one after another.

bodega: A small grocery store in an urban area, one usually specializing in Hispanic groceries.

choreography: The art of designing dances and movements.

coalition: A group of people or groups who've come together for a common purpose.

concept: Organized around a main idea or theme.

culture: The beliefs and ways of life of a certain group of people.

fantasy: Something produced by the imagination.

immigrant: A person who comes to a country to live there.

multicultural: Relating to or made up of several different cultures.

psychologist: A person who studies psychology, or the science that studies the mind and behavior.

rebellion: A fight to overthrow a government.

scholarship: Money given to someone to pay for school.

thrive: To grow successfully.

version: A form of something that is different from the ones that came before it.

INDEX

WEBSITES

Due to the changing nature of Internet links, PowerKids Press has
developed an online list of websites related to the subject of this book.
This site is updated regularly. Please use this link to access the list:
www.powerkidslinks.com/bbios/miranda